For Delia McAuliffe—

You share the secrets!

Mentor:
Secrets of the Ages

Copyright © 1981 by Art Fettig

All rights reserved. No part of this book may be reproduced or transmitted in any form or by any means, electronic or mechanical, including photocopying, recording or by any information storage and retrieval system, without permission in writing from the Publisher.

For information address:
Frederick Fell Publishers, Inc.
386 Park Avenue South
New York, New York, 10016

Library of Congress Catalog Card Number: 80-70956

International Standard Book Number: 0-8119-0333-8

1 2 3 4 5 6 7 8 9 0

Printed in the United States of America

OTHER BOOKS BY ART FETTIG

It Only Hurts When I Frown

Anatomy of a Speech

Selling Lucky, A Guide to Greater

Success and Happiness

How To Hold An Audience In The Hollow

Of Your Hand

The Three Robots

*I dedicate this book
to those who cried, or bled, or nodded,
or somehow let me realize
that they really understood.*

PREFACE

How can people hope to understand writers, when writers cannot understand themselves?

I wrote this book while traveling in Spain with my wife, Ruth, and my daughter, Amy. The book really wrote itself, I merely put it down on paper.

We were waiting in a railroad station in Madrid. Amy braved a long and unruly line for tickets, and rather than stand there waiting impatiently as my irritation grew, I took out a pad of paper, sat down on a suitcase and began to write.

Three days later, I spoke to Amy and Ruth again and tried to apologize to them for being such a miserable and inconsiderate traveling companion. The situation was beyond a mere apology. I don't believe that I will ever understand the spell that this story cast upon me. I do hope that one day Ruth and Amy read it.

As much as I write, I still cannot fathom the creative process. All I know is that this story was deep inside me and demanded to come out. I hope there are more like this in there.

—Art Fettig

Mentor:
Secrets of the Ages

—I—

WHERE DO YOU go after you've already been there again and again?

When you've been to the very top of the mountain and seen all there is to be seen?

When you've already drunk more than your measure of life and its joys?

That was the question. Edgar had searched for the answer again and again.

What do you seek when you've found all you searched for?

Edgar was a man who had studied success with a powerful microscope.

He had found the wisdom of the ages, by taking one upward journey after the other.

From poverty to untold wealth. From self-doubt to self-awareness. From loathing to acceptance, and then growth beyond the dream.

From hate, to a depth of love he could not comprehend. From sickness, both of mind and body, to a healthy glow, both from deep within and without.

From a dull stupor and the deepest ignorance of all, to a growing understanding of the universe and all its mysteries. To a knowledge of the secrets of the ages. He was at peace with both humankind and a Power above.

And yet, now sound of body, soul and mind, Edgar found himself knocking, as he had so many times before, on the door of Manfred, his mentor.

The men embraced and stood quietly sharing an inner glow that told each all was still quite well within their world.

Finally, Edgar posed the question that filled his thoughts. "Manfred, I do not wish to climb yet another mountain by myself. I've tasted joy so many times. What else is there for me?"

Manfred stood and studied his pupil. Then he broke the lengthy silence with a smile, and said, "I think the time has come for you to find true happiness, by sharing all you've learned with someone who has lost the way."

Looking into Edgar's eyes, Manfred continued, "Edgar, the total of your joy will be in direct proportion to the distance that you travel with the one with whom you choose to make the trip. Select a companion with but a little way to travel and meager will be your joy. Find a soul who must a mountain climb, and soon perhaps, your heart will overflow, or break, if as it might, your wisdom fails to help that soul pass the test.

There was no need for further small talk between the men, for they had to be about important tasks. Once more did they embrace, and both were filled with feelings few souls share.

Then Edgar was alone with yet another of the secrets of the ages.

Manfred's words began to echo in the chambers of his mind: "The total of your joy will be in direct proportion to the distance that you travel with the one with whom you choose to make the trip."

Edgar closed his eyes and saw in his mind's eye a hopeless derelict, a useless wreck of a man, with lice biting at his back, reeking from a stench both inside and outside his body.

This man was about as low as a human being could fall, and Edgar knew that that man was him, when first he met Manfred so many years before.

Suddenly it all became quite clear. Edgar knew the type of man he must see: a man as wretched and beaten as he once had been.

For now was the time for him to pass on that message of happiness and joy he had learned.

Soon, he would know the meaning of the joy of giving.

—II—

Bradford Wellington the Third thought he'd died. And he wished he had, for there was almost nothing left of him. He couldn't weigh a hundred pounds.

He'd gone bankrupt—financially, mentally, and physically—and now he wasn't even sure there was a God. But God, (or someone else above), how he needed just one drink to ease him through his final hour on Earth.

Then he'd end it all and cease to be a burden on the world.

He looked up from his sullen sorrow. Certainly somewhere in the night there must be one kind soul, who might a dollar spare, to ease his pain.

Brad brushed away the matted hair that fell across his troubled face. One kind samaritan, who for just one fleeting instant might comprehend the agony that filled his soul, and lend, mind you not give but lend a dollar for a temporary loan.

Where was that soul out there among the darkness? Why didn't God or someone else up there send down a light so that he might find the solace that he craved?

Then a kindly looking soul approached, and yes, he seemed to Brad to wear both an inner and outer glow. 'Twas Edgar, out in search of such a soul as Bradford Wellington the Third.

—III—

EDGAR STARED AT Bradford Wellington the Third for a full moment. He saw the ruin of a man who certainly was suffering the agonies of Hell. How well he knew those feelings. A man doesn't forget, though he may try.

Edgar reached out and took the beaten man into his arms. "We'll travel from here to there together now. Come, my friend," said Edgar.

Brad stretched out a grimy hand. "Just a dollar, man, to ease my pain and then I will not burden you, or anyone again. A dollar, and you may forget I passed your way."

"Oh no," Edgar cried. "I cannot forget you now. I need you for my future. Can't you see I've sought you out?"

That was something Bradford Wellington the Third simply could not comprehend. Before, he had seen shunned by all he met.

It must be his drunkenness that let him dream some other human cared. And yet, this person stayed and did not run.

"A dollar, just a dollar, sir—to ease my pain and help me to forget my circumstances."

But no, the dollar did not come. And the stranger waited by his side.

Edgar sat down on the bench beside the wreck and said, "I want to help you. I want to bring you back among the living and show you how to fill your life with joy."

Brad laughed a hopeless laugh. He whined pleadingly, for he was now not beyond most anything. "For God's sake man, to hell with joy. Just help me buy that bottle which will ease my pain!"

Edgar nodded. "A bottle, yes, if that is how we must begin. But let me take you to my home and there we will embark upon a journey to a life for you. I have traveled down this road myself, and now we'll take those steps together."

"Riddles," Brad thought, "useless riddles are what this man gives me." All his body craved was one more drink, and let it be his last, and then he'd end it all, but no. The stranger took his arm and Brad was too weak to tell him, "No." Or to bid him, "Go."

They walked, or staggered if you will, and hailed a cab, and rode until the fare seemed like a fortune. With the fare alone, Brad could have drunk himself insensible for weeks.

Soon, the cab was in the driveway of what surely must be the mansion of a wealthy man. And well it was, for Edgar lived a life of luxury, since he had climbed the mountain of success so many times.

They went inside, Edgar poured a potion, and Bradford Wellington the Third drank to the bottom of the glass, drifting to a restful sleep.

— IV —

THE DAYS PASSED, painfully to start.

Edgar gave him broth at first, and then a full-bodied soup. In a week, he began to eat food that was solid, and Brad passed first one day, and then a week, without a drink.

Antabuse provided the incentive not to drink at first, for just the hint of alcohol made Brad quite ill for hours. At last, because of all the words of wisdom Edgar spoke, Brad had the will to live, and now they started out to build a life for him.

The first lesson Edgar taught was the one that Manfred first taught him so many years before:

SET A GOAL.

A goal that, while being quite worthwhile, was short term, plausible, and quite well within reach. One must build a history of success if success is yet to fill one's life. And so, together, they set a simple common goal: to take that body still so frail and build it up so that it might survive.

They started with a high-carbohydrate diet, and soon the ribs were not so evident. The color bloomed again upon Brad's cheeks.

He would survive, without alcohol. His mind began to heal, too. Soon there was a smile upon the face of Bradford Wellington the Third.

He stopped that awful stooping, and for once, he stood erect. Chest out, head high, shoulders back. The first time he tried it, how it hurt his back! But now, with practice, Brad could do it for hours. Every now and then, that smile returned—how it felt foreign upon his face.

For once, he faced a mirror without shuddering, because Edgar had repeated and repeated that he was a worthwhile man who soon would grow to taste the joy of living. Once he had learned the formula of winning.

And win they did.

His weight returned. This time, not a bloated paunch, but as the result of their daily hikes, good flesh, with muscles all around.

He almost liked himself. He almost thought there was hope.

Somehow, he had done it all without a drink.

True, it was just an hour at a time sometimes, but already he was thinking of a whole day at a time and that was quite enough to lead a hopeful life.

One day at a time.

—V—

Now HIS EDUCATION would begin.

Edgar took him to a meeting of A.A. (Alcoholics Anonymous). Brad laughed. Just how anonymous did he seem to be when in the gutter he lay? It wasn't anonymity he sought, but sanity, and serenity, and purpose. There he found all three.

He learned that he was sick. Not bad. Not rotten through and through, as he had thought. But sick.

And he could be quite well again, if only he would make it through each day without a drink.

It did not seem all that bad, for Edgar went along to all those meetings. And he talked as if he'd suffered from these symptoms, too.

I fear that we have painted much too bright a picture here. And now like artists, we must back away and view just what we've done. It's much too plain, we've failed to sketch the pain and suffering that our Bradford did endure.

He retched and retched some more. He pounded on the door and begged for just one more drink. He crawled—oh yes, he crawled across the floor and tried the door with the hope he could escape.

But all of that passed. Now, our Bradford Wellington the Third was fast upon the road to his recovery.

Time passes slowly with an empty glass.

So, one day at a time, the men discussed good living.

—VI—

How can a man, aged thirty-five, suddenly come alive and find that he is in search of a philosophy?

Brad could remember, from somewhere in his past, the words, that he believed in the Lord God, Almighty, and in Jesus Christ, the only son of our Lord. But all he could associate with this was that on Sunday he should go to church. And when waking with a woman, there was such a sense of guilt.

Somehow, he recalled, religion had gone away those years he spent in college, while he was managing to, sometimes, sober up enough to cram for tests.

When he finally received his bachelor's degree, he put it in a safe deposit vault and drifted on. He'd worked a lot at jobs, quite fancy at the start, and near the end at anything that he could find, to raise enough for one more drink.

He never taught, though teaching was the only thing he thought he'd like. He'd studied with that occupation on his mind, but never set a goal before.

Now his goal was merely to stay alive for one more day.

And the days went past.

—VII—

EDGAR BOUGHT a little here, a little there. Daily presents, one might say, until within a month, he'd bought a simple wardrobe for his new-found friend. It was a vast improvement over the tattered jeans and ragged shirt he'd found Bradford Wellington the Third in.

A barber worked a minor miracle, too.

As his weight increased, Brad found the courage to take pen in hand and write a goal that somehow caused his steady hand to tremble.

"I will find a job . . ." he wrote, and after mindful contemplation added, ". . . teaching."

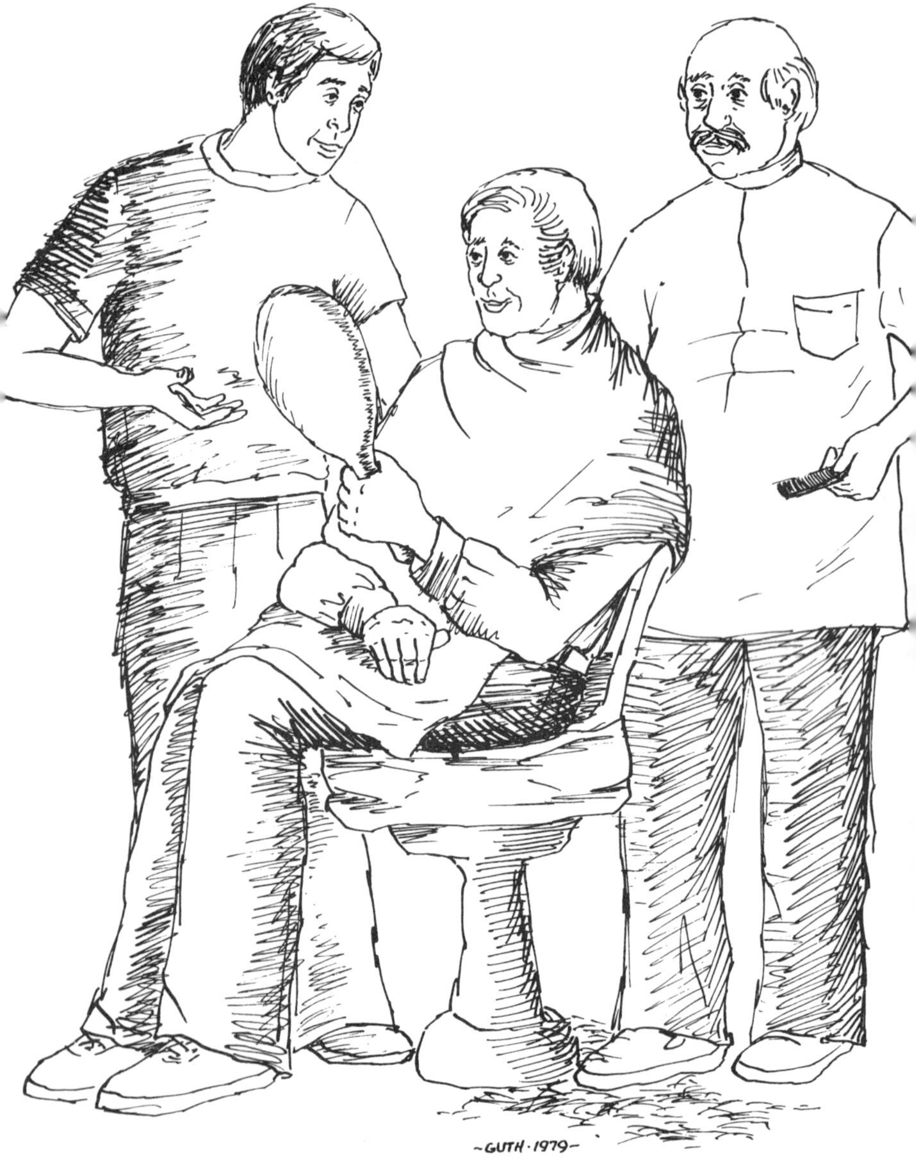
~GUTH·1979~

With all his influence and power, Edgar certainly could have made a call and found a way. But this was not to be, for it was time for Bradford Wellington the Third to learn another principle of living.

It seemed so obvious when Edgar first explained it, yet all his life, Brad had functioned in the opposite fashion.

"To increase your opportunities, increase your circle of friends." How often in his lifetime, when opportunities did not smile his way, Bradford Wellington the Third had said, "You have to know somebody in this world." But he had never thought to make new friends.

Edgar explained. "For opportunity to smile your way, it must at least know you are alive."

—VIII—

So BRAD WENT back to the university from whence he'd picked up his degree, and then he talked and talked, and then he listened for a change. Conversation soon became his full-time occupation—at least until a job might come his way.

"Experience?"

He thought of just inventing a new past to cover up the life he'd thrown away. But somehow he could not create what never was.

He filled out applications 'til his writing hand ached, and yet it seemed to no avail. He took out ads and made a daily chore of trying every door that he might find, and finally, before despair engulfed him, he just went to work.

He had no job, but something Edgar said began to settle in the cobwebs of his mind, "If you seek a job, go do it. Later you can work out details."

So one morning, bright and early, Bradford Wellington III simply walked into a classroom and began.

Of course, there was an instructor there already, and so at first, Brad merely sat and watched. What evolved seemed like a folly.

No one was learning a thing, it seemed, and no one cared.

What a waste, those minds unchallenged. Yet, as he recalled, he was the same way when he was a senior in high school. Back then, girls and drinking beer were all that occupied his mind.

The worn professor had given up so long ago, and now he merely made his daily presence known, and resigned himself to pacifying his charges with anything that somehow might occupy their time. It was a restless class. It seemed as if not one there had the slightest concept of what economics meant. Most of the professor's time was spent just trying to control the restless mob.

Then one day the teacher did not come and everyone assumed that Bradford Wellington the Third would soon be heard mouthing phrases from the regular professor. But alas, Brad faced the class and soon began to empty his soul.

"This is a crime, what's happening each day within this room," he cried out. "Let us begin to study economics. But forget your books. We'll write our own. Let us begin by figuring the cost of every moment that you waste today."

It was a revolutionary thought. Moments with value? If that were true, then collectively they were squandering a fortune every day.

They added up the moments of the class and set a goal to somehow make those moments earn their keep.

"Rule one for life," Bradford Wellington the Third began. "Pay yourself first from every dollar you receive."

And then, as if by fate, the teacher stayed away, and within a week they'd traveled to the bank and forty-five new bank accounts appeared. "Pay yourself first, at least a tenth of what you earn, and soon you will accumulate a stake," said Brad.

When Brad began conducting the class, his students stayed away as often as they came to occupy their desk. Now they clustered in the classroom, and if just one were absent, others called them to see if they had found some misfortune.

The class was a team, and now it budgeted together a great savings. Within a month, Brad had faced the school administrators and found acceptance in their ranks.

He was employed. And overjoyed.

Now it was Bradford Wellington the Third, the *teacher,* talking of a place to call his own. "To grow you must take risks," Edgar had told him repeatedly. Yes, it was so wonderful to stay with Edgar at his home, and yet growing demanded that Brad take this step.

"To grow you must take risks." So, Bradford Wellington the Third packed up his new-won wardrobe and moved into a tiny room near the school.

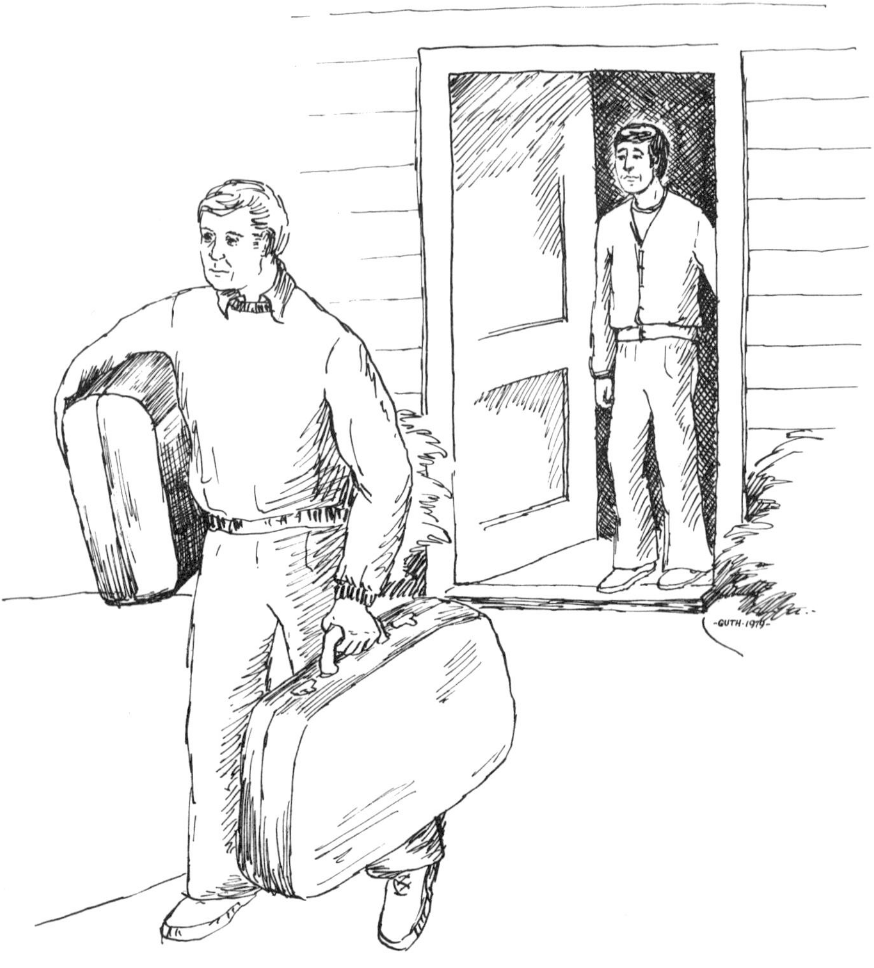
-GUTH-1979-

What fool would leave the comfort of dear Edgar's spacious home for such a place? A fool who felt the need to grow. And grow he did.

—IX—

BRAD BEGAN to explore both his conscious and unconscious mind. Somehow, now, he viewed it as a precious tool that would serve him well.

He studied the human brain and wondered how his own had gone astray from alcohol. He learned about the wondrous chambers of his mind. Among them, his memory, wherein was stored the garbage that had made him feel that once he was a worthless being.

Now he did believe that if he might just master the mystery of his mind, he would become a true success. His mind could lead to the redemption of his very being.

First he worked on memory. In the past, names were insignificant to him. Who cared who was who back then? It didn't matter in the least. People came and went quickly, and few left anything worthwhile in Bradford's life. So he never bothered with collecting names. Numbers were what people were today. Holes in computer cards that some cold and rapid machine would process and then file.

If people did not know their own names that was their problem, not his.

But now, as he examined this in depth, he learned that to some, their name was their most priceless inheritance. The dearest thing that they possessed. And some would gladly die to preserve the honor of their name. To some it meant that much.

In his search, Bradford Wellington the Third stumbled on an ancient memory book and soon discovered that memory could be learned. It was a science. He worked on names—of the members of his class, for instance. Soon he knew them all by name and they learned his name, too. He learned to look at people's faces and soon discovered each and every one unique.

Names took on new meaning. Nationalities emerged. Histories. Roots. Reasons for conversation.

Then Brad studied numbers and, working with the ancient memory book, evolved a system of memory pegs that enabled him to lock in information that before had been impossible for him to cope with. The reserve potential of the human brain nearly took his breath away.

And he understood why up to now he had been functioning at a small percentage of his true capacity. Memory? Why it was such a joyous game that heretofore in life he simply had not learned to play.

He tried poetry and discovered that it came quite easily now with the memory system. Numbers, faces, names, lists, and speeches. Why, he had the Constitution down cold with just one evening's effort.

The mind. What else was up there unexplored? His mind was swelling with new-found wisdom.

Next Bradford Wellington the Third explored his attitude. Why did it fluctuate so? Some mornings he was up there with the eagles soaring and the world was bright and round and full of promise. Other days were black and full of gloom.

Was this thing called "attitude" something he might control?

He pondered, he examined, and he found a few who appeared to him to be right up there flying with those eagles every day.

"How do you keep your mood up there, every single day?" he asked them.

Some shrugged and said, "Why not?" One vibrant, merry man told Bradford Wellington the Third his secret, and it stuck there in Brad's mind: "I control my thoughts. I control my destiny. I control my moods. I can be happy every day or miserable, you see. It's up to me. I put those feelings in my mind."

Brad tried it. Caring for and feeding his subconscious mind only happy, positive, enthusiastic thoughts and then he told his mind to put a smile upon his lips.

Smiling felt clumsy, at first, to a man who wore a frown so many many years. The lips felt twisted and out of shape. The reactions that his new-found smile inspired startled him at first.

With frowning, people turned away, or frowned back, or scowled. People avoid a forever-frowning person. Solitude comes easy. And loneliness too.

But Bradford Wellington the Third discovered when he wore a friendly smile, people smiled back. It seemed infectious. He'd been wasting valuable energy on frowning. Frowning used thirty-seven muscles and smiling only five. Smiling was such an easy thing now; now and then his smile was returned by someone with a friendly word.

Yes, he soon discovered that a positive attitude could change his world. And with his bright new attitude ambition pulsed within him.

Soon he had a tutor's job to fill his evening hours. Edgar understood and cheered him on.

Each Saturday they met and talked for hours, and Bradford Wellington the Third listened, and he learned the lessons that he took back to his classroom. And his classes thrived.

Bradford soon increased the circles of his friendships, for his students took him home with them. Their families became his friends. Next, he started selling an encyclopedia; how his savings grew!

"The Professor" they all called him, and he walked erect and smiled and felt a new-found comfort in his soul.

Brad found a woman friend to share a quiet cup of tea. A second woman baked him cakes and brought them to his room. But nothing lasting developed, for he felt it was too soon.

He wanted so to grow. How he wanted to grow. And grow he did, for each of his students set a weekly goal. And how they grew.

With the books he sold, Brad used a loving hand, matching needed knowledge with each seeking mind and how his profits grew.

Somehow he got back to God, and now he prayed. And every day he exercised his body and his mind with wisdom that dear Edgar shared. How he grew in body, mind and soul!

Edgar soon began to know the joy of helping another grow, and he thrived, too.

—X—

WHEN SUMMER CAME, the students in Bradford's class moved on, for they had all found risks to take themselves. As they parted each embraced their teacher, for they knew that because he touched their lives, they were wiser.

Now it was time to take still greater risks, and Bradford bought some income property. Through the summer days he toiled, and soon his tenants carried expense of the building.

As Bradford Wellington the Third toiled, he discovered that the key to enjoying every form of labor was in striving to excel, no matter what the chore; endeavoring to improve on the result each time he tried. The secret to enjoying any job lay in doing it the very best he could. With this knowledge he could tackle almost any type of labor with true gusto.

Before August, he had his second place. He'd work eight hours, sell books four more, and he succeeded. He taught and reinvested time again, and selling came much easier to him, and how he thrived.

When he felt the time was right he found and took a loving wife, Marie. With his wife beside him, Bradford Wellington the Third unwound a little. And he learned to laugh. Out loud, in front of everyone.

A sense of humor. What a new dimension this was to Brad's developing personality. He studied humor and he learned that somehow the ability to take his work seriously and himself lightly eased the pressure that sometimes came with business and with the business of success. Humor let him look at things different ways.

Humor taught him about opposites.

He soon observed that humor was thinking bigger than and smaller than and differently. As his sense of humor developed, he observed how humor added to his perception. Suddenly he could see through things and better see things through.

He could now examine a problem from a variety of angles, from a whole new point of view. His vision took on an omnipotence, and seeing the other person's point of view allowed him to get nearer to the truth of a situation than most people ever approach.

Humor released the tension in his life.

He could laugh a bellowing laugh and find renewal, and insight, and comfort. Some say he laughed his way to greatness.

Humor had added a dimension of optimism. While the laughing didn't always change the problems, it did help him to live with them.

Then humor helped him ease the pain of all his yesteryears. Somehow it let him put his former useless life into its true perspective, and with time he learned to laugh out loud about his drunken past. Without crying.

Bradford Wellington the Third learned a certain playfulness in life and now his work became a greater joy. Marie shared his growth and grew with him. And they were such a loving pair.

Now all this while he kept alert for growth of mind, body, and soul. And he continued to set goals and he continued to achieve them. And then one day he dreamed.

—XI—

EDGAR HAD TOLD him about dreaming.

Dreaming was a bit more difficult than mere goal setting. Dreaming made you let your spirit soar. And Bradford Wellington the Third closed his eyes, leaned back, and dreamed a healthy, daring dream.

When he had his dream in place, he went to Edgar so he might take the necessary step to make his dream come true. He listened so attentively as Edgar explained to him the rules.

Yes, he had the dream fixed firmly in his mind. His loving wife, Marie, by his side, at the door of their beautiful new home. A car, a very wonderful car in their driveway. And a healthy son, too.

He visualized every detail, and wrote it down boldly for Edgar to see. It was necessary that he share this dream with another individual. To it all he fixed a date, and then he acted as if it had all come true.

And within a year it had.

His son thrived, the parents' love grew, and they had it all together.

In haste, I fear I made it all too simple. Let us take a finer brush and stroke in more detail.

But no, the secret to success is not as complicated as those who fail would make it.

True, I didn't tell you of how Bradford Wellington the Third fixed broken toilets in the old apartments that he bought. Or how he courted all in vain, but lost, but won at last because he found Marie, a far more loving person.

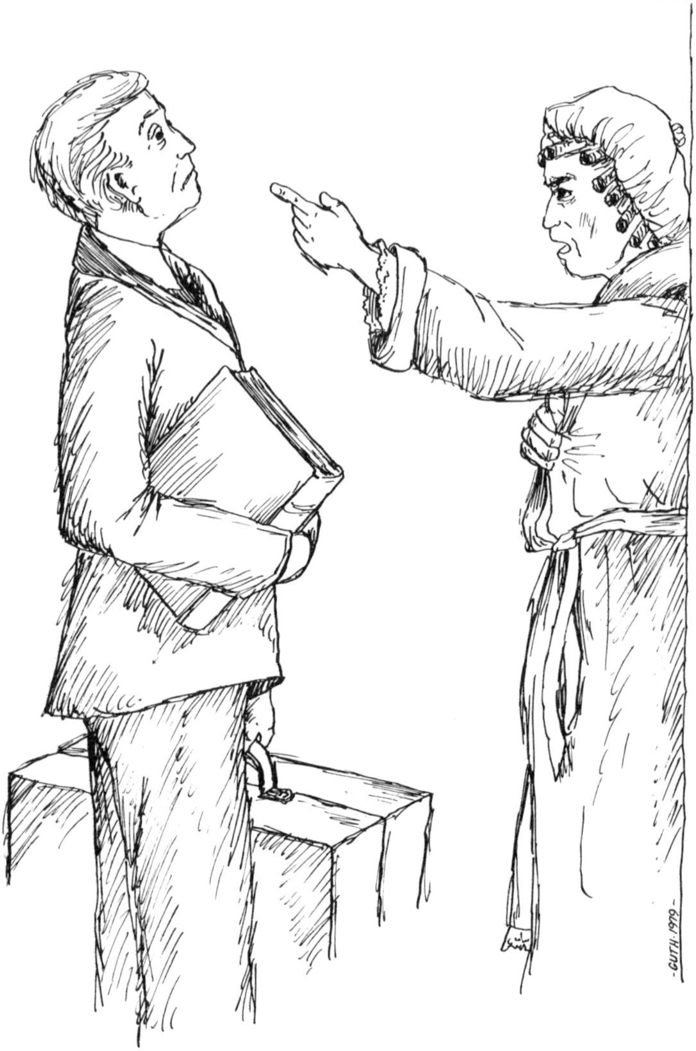
-GUTH.1979-

I didn't tell about collecting rents, or how so many didn't buy those heavy books he carted to their homes.

I find I only told you of the progress that he made, and not the pain. For ours is just the story of how one man grew.

And growth does not transpire without a wealth of pain.

—XII—

OFTEN BRADFORD WELLINGTON the Third would fall upon the ground because the pain of mind, body and soul nearly overcame him, but he'd lift his head and cry out, "I'm growing, yes, I'm growing, for I feel that awful pain."

Then one day old Manfred passed on. Edgar cried, and Bradford by his side shared his sorrow. And as they parted, Bradford Wellington the Third began to think.

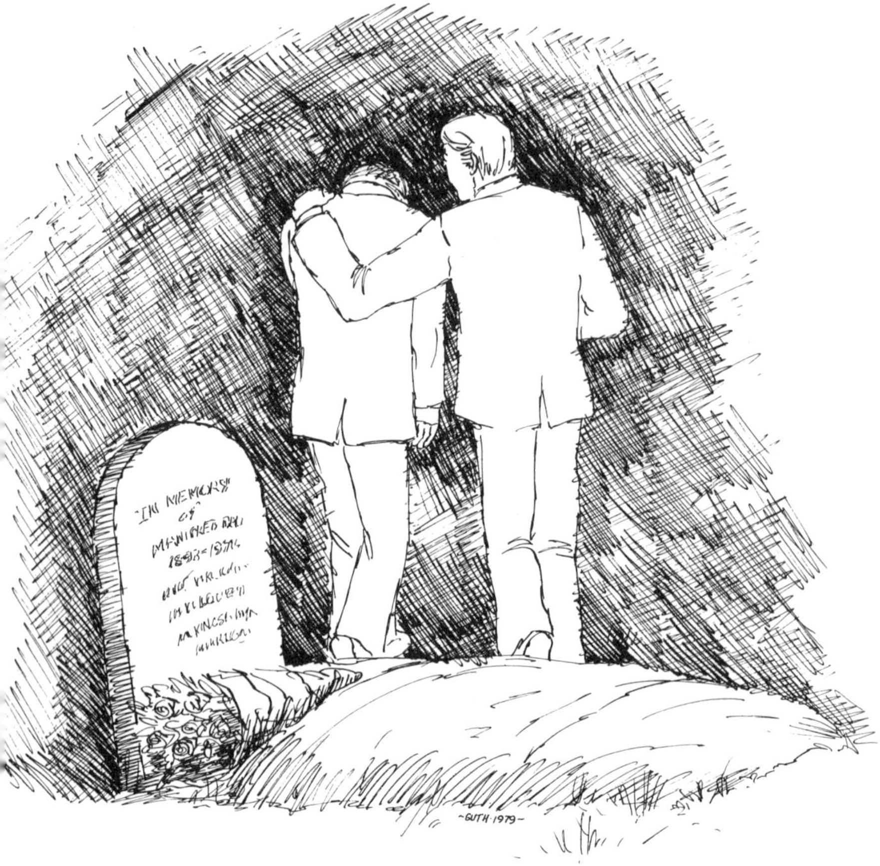
"IN MEMORY
OF
-GUTH·1979-

Later when he talked a while to Edgar, he knew what he must do. He heard it echo in the chambers of his mind. It was a message Edgar had passed along to him at his request.

"You must find a soul that must a mountain climb. And soon perhaps your heart will overflow, or break, if as it might, your wisdom fails to help that soul pass the test."

Bradford Wellington the Third walked the streets alone, seeking a wretched soul. The words of Edgar rang through his mind. "The total of your joy will be in direct proportion to the distance that you travel with the one with whom you choose to make the trip."

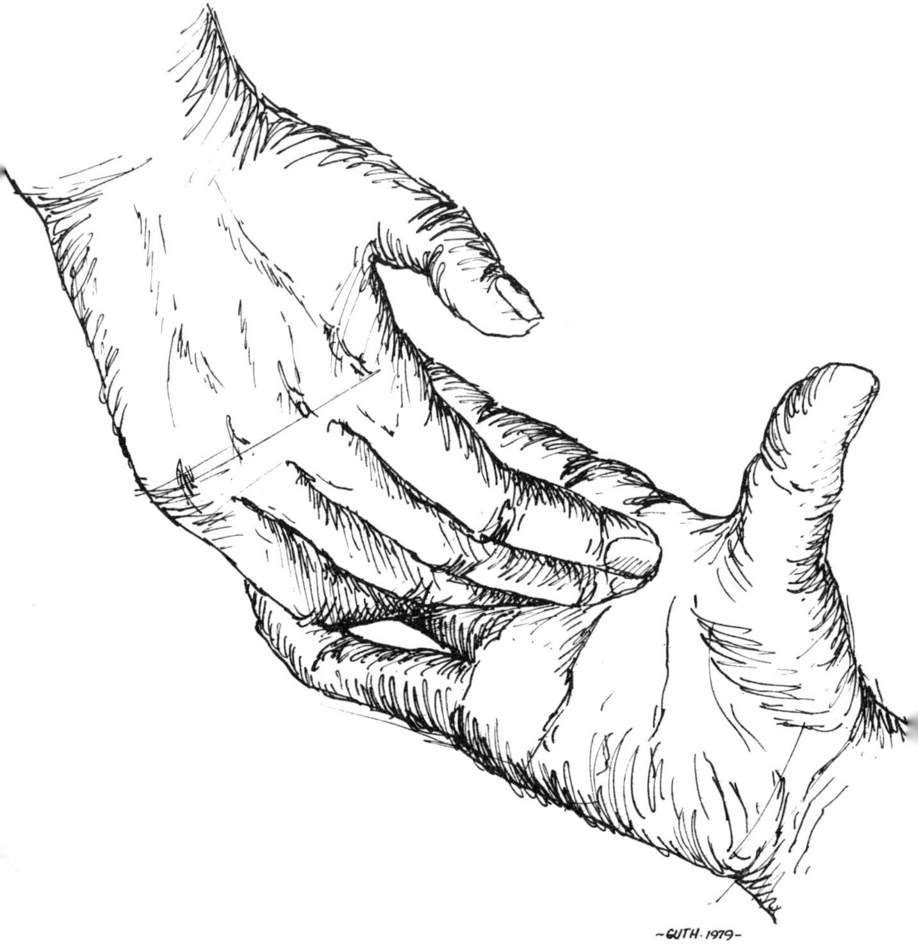
~GUTH. 1979~

Bradford searched the streets, and then the gutters, 'til he found me.

And I begged him for a bottle. But he gave me love.

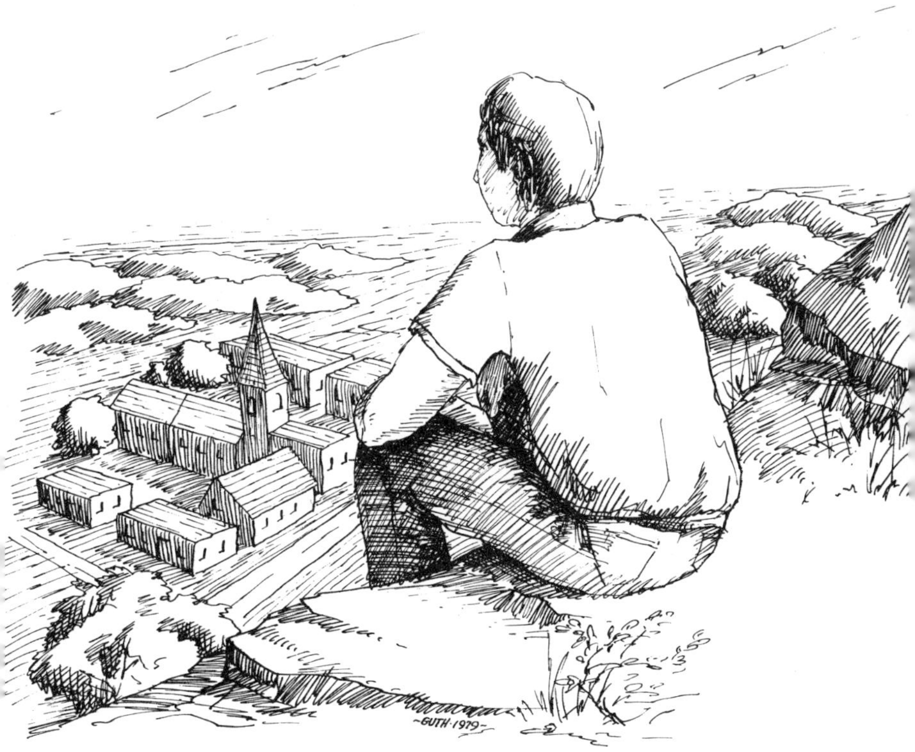
~GUTH·1979~